MW00477125

The
Squanicook Eclogues

W · W · NORTON & COMPANY

New York · London

The Squanicook Eclogues

Melissa Green

Grateful acknowledgment is made to *The Agni Review* in which an earlier draft of "The Squan-icook Eclogues" appeared. Special thanks to The Townsend Historical Society, Townsend, Massachusetts, and Pamela Dodds for the cover photo; and to Rosanna Warren for her generous support.

Cover painting by Rufus Porter.

Copyright © 1987 by Melissa Green
All rights reserved.
Published simultaneously in Canada by Penguin Books Canada Ltd., 2801 John Street, Markham, Ontario L3R 1B4.
Printed in the United States of America.

The text of this book is composed in Garamond, with display type set in Garamond Old Style. Composition and manufacturing by The Maple-Vail Book Manufacturing Group.
Book design by Antonina Krass.

First Edition

3 3309 00042 5187

ISBN 0-393-02455-5 NBZI

W. W. Norton & Company, Inc., 500 Fifth Avenue, New York, N. Y. 10110
W. W. Norton & Company Ltd., 37 Great Russell Street, London WC1B 3NU

1 2 3 4 5 6 7 8 9 0

FOR GEORGE WEBBER

Contents

I

The
Squanicook Eclogues

for Richard Winthrop Green, Jr.

April

After a blustery, fretful March, the fields have yawned,
Tossing off their goosedown coverlets to thaw.
In airing upstairs farmhouse rooms, the sunlight paints
A sudden gold-leaf on the dresser drawers and wall.
In his oldest jacket, I wade the oxen road,
And under my boots, a gingery leaf-fall breeds new growth
Beside the crooked stone fence bordering two states.
Heaved by frost, it holds its steady, snakelike course,
And now it's dappled in a shadblow's oval shade.
Brush-marked by spring, the sodden alfalfa is brassy with birds.
Hundreds forage in bleached reeds, robins and starlings,
Striking like fired shafts from a branch's shuddering bow.
Beneath the russet mulch and leaves, a culvert floods
An aisle transfusing tender pergolas of grapes.
Clouds from the south scallop an altarcloth made by nuns,
And the loyal brass horse reels on the ridgepole spindle.

My father chose the iconography of trees
Instead of church, and on those Sundays, served the Truce
Of God. No argument divided us except
A war of grapes. What light artillery escaped
His lips was whistling so peaceful that it seemed
A sparrow's furtive mourning from its book of psalms,
Intended for the breeze alone; in spring, his scythe
Was steel instead of words. Chaotic April seethed,
In ruthless disregard for boundaries, across
Our forty-acre farm, a hummock at the crest
Of Barker Hill. Below, an amphitheater-wide
And far into the valley from our northern woods,
A granite quarry like an ancient city slept
Submerged, and bright with runoff from Monadnock's slopes,
The drifting ash a hundred Januarys' snow.
Its wagonwheels were buried driftwood half-moons now.
And farther, past a line of conifer, the town
Lay huddled, unaware we watched, its houses strewn
Along the spongy inlets of the Squanicook.

The shadblow's white five-petaled stars have dropped in snow.
Elliptical bursts of bright green chevrons fan the air.
Along the wall, the linden fills with heart-shaped leaves,
Palmately-veined, serrated, pale and olive green.
The willow is a yellow prairie sundress, fat
With catkins, a woman in a rocker shelling beans.
The maple's clustered fountain-jets of blood have splayed
In short-lobed leaves, the stenciled veins of stubby hands.
In alfalfa, spiders have labored to weave the peat-rich air
Into goldenrod, daisy, geranium, trillium, lily, phlox.
Tentative teaberry rings its bell-shaped blooms.
Anemone quinquefolia fans attenuate stalks
Beside unfurling bloodroot, surrendering its white
Flags, a virgin banner on an emerald field.

The river dwellers claimed her: Eostre's men who caulk
Piazzas and their bulkhead doors; the boys who thrust
Aluminum canoes through currents past their wrists
In summer; widows' mottled ornamental ducks,
Oblivious to light from either equinox,
Reflecting gravely on their sluggish, perfect forms,
A travesty of Eden's flocks; eroding farms;
Displaced Triptolemus who wandered west and died.
Such an intermingling of dreams the brook endowed.

v *Water*

Father, I'm drowsy in April's humming sun and think
A girl the color of autumn kneels at the Squanicook's bank,
Who is the river's daughter, dressed in driven skins,
Who knows a cedar wind at Nissequassick brings
The schools of alewife, herring, yellow perch ashore.
The Place of Salmon roars with light. She steps, sure-
Footed onto stone; lithe as a poplar, bends over
The water. Wren feathers, shells, seven quills quiver
In her sable hair. Her eyes, a spring-fed stream,
Like silica, seek bottom. Deep in her mossy brain,
The white-tailed mouse is born. She carries in her supple
Body all of spring—a tree frog in the apple,
A kit fox dozing in the brush, a brash otter
Diving her river-veins—the new, young, utterly
Green morning beads her skin. How simply she leans
Into understanding, baptized by light and the delicate lines
Of shadow from cedar. A goldfinch has flown its ribbed nest,
Dusting her cheek with its wing, a hummingbird throbs in her
                                                    wrist,
She is drenched in waking. Wonder, a long-legged doe,
Drinks in deeply, as all instinctive creatures do,
And laughs, leaping the current, printing the field with dew.

August

I thread the blackberry thicket for the shaded stone.
August has shriven the grass, the green sargassos of June,
And summer's alfalfa is lusterless gold in a nimbus of heat
Waiting the baler. It wavers, helpless, a phalanx of light.
August drums as bright thunder trumpets the field,
And the maple's khaki undersides lift in a brisk salute
To shadows stalled against the pitiless scope of the sun.
Rain will riddle the valley, strafing blistered grains,
And black-eyed Susans in unison rise like the girls of St. Anne's.
Where foxglove in her petticoat has crowned the hill—
An indolent cotillion girl who tosses gold
From her shoulders, and proudly rustles yards of crinoline—
Freckled goldenrod assembles, choir boys,
A drift of anise, bobbing over their schoolyard gate.
A sunflower's ovate leaves become the rough arms
Of a drowsy fieldhand, leaning on a split-rail fence,
Whose mouse-brown eye, alerted, lashed with gold, translates
The clouds as victory, the wind's voice as rain.

I knew the river wasn't theirs at all. Just once
When January sun on snow had made us wince,
When hickory and juniper were frosted cakes
On Barker Hill, my father tracked the Squanicook
With one gloved hand above the valley's heart—a braid
Of shattered mirrors bridging fields and barns and roads,
Through yards resigned to her encyclical despair.
In watching shards fragment those stalwart gabled spires,
I saw a fractured picture of our town and knew
I heard an ancient, urgent fury break the snow,
A fierce quicksilvering of winter's crusted dyke.
I watched it runnel gently where we crouched; its wake
Defied the valley, joyfully sped from where we gazed.
I felt the shrugging off of nature's deep disguise.
The river favored us. She lived and leapt the gorge.

The shadblow sheds its purple fruit and spills its seed,
The linden bartering yellow bouquets for a necklace of gourds.
Unbraided pennons, catkins of the willow, fill
Like ragged sails. A towering cumulonimbus patrols
The eastern skies. I watch magenta clover drone
On sleeping epaulettes and know the sun-soaked earth
Is breeding still: in torpid pools, in stagnant ponds,
Rebellious nature sets her offspring quarreling
For food and territory—in-bred stone-flies riot
For their rations where the water striders run
Their useless marathons; inflammatory toads
Attempt a revolution, all in vain. In time,
The planet's microcosmic battles merge and fail,
Leaves of drying blood consumed, a season's compost.

iv

We walked the property a thousand times, as if
Without our walking there, the landscape might dissolve.
His trees were young. A drought-summer spark had cleared
The western third some time ago, and when he could,
He meant to have that forest back. He planted spruce
The size of children's pencils, fifteen hundred sprays
Of evergreen, each year as spindly as the last.
It hurt to watch him tearing up the ones he'd lost.
We carried water from the brook sometimes. It sluiced
A dozen clotted paths, where once an ancestor sliced
The forest open, and oxen, yoked, had dragged a road.
This was ours. New Hampshire, north of us, was broad
And diffident as France. With vague disdain, at six,
I knew our woods were better—even my burdocked socks
Belonged to Massachusetts. And I loved our field
Whose hundred-year-old hair had not been cut; it filled
With captivated birds. A thorny orchard kept
A dozen wizards prisoner. I watched their script
Of runes engrave the granite sky with ancient debt.
Everything the woods could teach, my father taught:
Delight, exactitude, a faith, his journeyman's doubt.

v *Fire*

Father, I'm dizzy in shimmering August, rising new
As summer's mistress from a field of corn. She now
Is married to the heat-swept grain. Her ripening breast
Is a thicket, bright with blood-berries, her body dressed
In flame. The red god of the salamander sandals her foot,
A monarch touches her lip, her coppery hands fit
Petals in a chain. She knows she has chosen to burn
At noon, as nature intends. The thrust maize, unborn,
Has made her heavy and drugged as a bee. A tawny wood-
Dove sleepily croons what her tongue cannot: the subtle wound
That too much plenty makes. She doesn't know that winter
Ravages, that grief and habitual wind will tint her
Skin and break the tender stalk of her body. She stands
Impaled by arrows of afternoon light until thunder stuns
Her— she slips like smoke into shade, behind the burning stones.

October

  i   *from the sketchbook*

An early frost has lathered alfalfa's stubbled cheek,
The oxen road crunching like bacon under the creak of my boots.
Another flawless Sunday in October, clear,
Crisp, a pure sky plumed at the border by woodsmoke
And pagan banners of trees beguiling Protestant spires.
All the harvest has come down the valley: shelves
Protesting under bushel baskets, barn after barn.
The staghorn sumac rears its bloody hooves against
The ell where grapevine bickers with its shadow self.
Ceremonious maples don the cardinal robes of kings
While the dowager dogwood embroiders her taffeta cape.
Two starlings quarrel in an alder's blazing arc,
And for a moment, all the trees are winged, as if
In rousing autumn, a thousand bright tanagers, tiered,
Ruffled their breast feathers, calling. They cannot settle here.
Across the bronze medallion, dusk, a skein of scarves
Draws the wild geese over, audibly mourning, hoarse,
High wings turning the wheel of our envy, our grief.

                    2 I

More than novelty crooked its finger—silent, austere,
Deeper than trees beating their wings or the purblind stare
Of a black snake circumscribing a sapling's wrist.
Father carefully penciled facts, describing rust,
Habitat, genus, disease, but his meticulous chart
Of change didn't teach me to name the woods' mysterious heart.
Father, I'm frightened. Why are things so beautiful and sad?
My voice had dusted moss, like snow, without a sound.
Stern and tall, he cupped his chin. As if in pain
He paused, then reached into his pocket for a pen.
Don't ever make things up. Write only what you see.
Name the woods and you'll have named the world, he said.
He tore some pages off and handed me his pad.
I heard the current crimp, mimetic, on the pond,
And larch or beech or birds murmuring over me. The task
Was how to write *birch* when I saw the crumbling, pale tusk
Of a fallen mastodon bridging the path, or *ash,* when the air
Was frenzied with the head of a neighbor's rain-black mare.
Sycamore waved at me like drowned Ophelia's hair.

The shadblow shivers like a saved corsage, bronze
And apricot powder dusting every palsied leaf.
A spinster of chicory fearfully clasps a lilac stalk
With virginal fringe, guarding her single-day's bloom.
The clans convene: more coarsely toothed, in heart-shaped leaves,
Resilient, wrinkled aster skirts a hardihood,
The meadow filled with cousins who were towheads once;
Canadian thistle resisting a curvature of spine
Beside a boggy culvert; boneset, crowds of dock,
Replacing ragweed neighborhoods with random vetch.
A westerly wind shuffles the linden's pack of cards,
Held in age-spotted hands at a hennaed game of whist.
Witch hazel, worried by a joiner's planing hand,
Uncurls its shavings, branched like dowsers' wands, in vees.

iv

Something stirred from sleep as we passed by. It woke
And shook itself, I saw it light the linden's wicks
And heard it leafing through a coded archive, heard
An earth-brown collared killdeer beat its feathers, hard.
I knew the spirit of a thousand seasons rose
To welcome us, so long in coming through the trees.

v *Earth*

Father, leaves she's sent out from her leather hand,
A skulk of foxes, cannot turn the hunter's hounds.
October's temperamental wind, which burned to seize
The tamarack and rowan by their bridles, sighs
Because they're fetlock-deep in thorns. She is so old.
She can't outlast the transpiration of her blood.
And from a fire-fed bough, its flame, an ember the color
Of lynx, she's a bruised husk shaking the woods, a collar
Of yellow corn crowning her shoulder. Her fingers fret
Her belly, a swelled calabash that bears its fruit
Too late. She rests her cornucopia in frost
To sweep the chaff away, too tired to protest
The vagrant beggary of bats, the fossiled sky.
Her limbs erupt in ivy's epochal decay.
What is a body but a bier? Or suffering but love?
She gathers cones for her own barrow, takes down leaves,
And like the marrow-colored moon in clouds will guard
The huddled valley's harvest of beliefs. A gourd's
Faint staving-off of evil is rattling for God.

January

i *from the sketchbook*

The jays are commissars in uniform that rule
By evolution's ordinance. Its lesser birds
Survive haphazardly: the wrens are refugees,
And robins following the railroad south have veered
Toward destitution's camp, where fields are deeply scrolled
And hushed by January's harsh regime, and skies
Consolidate to cobalt under tungsten clouds.
A stenciling of dendrites drawn in photogravure
Has marred the gray horizon. Now consumptive twigs
Display disease and poverty across its screen.
In drifts, the muffled trees like soldiers shake their coats,
Elbowed in bark as in gabardine, and curse the wind,
Rabbits fraying their cuffs, trailing threads away.
The valley's shadows dust the snow with powder blue.
A crow concealed in arborvitae gives the charge,
And thorns like firing pins repeat it, lifted limbs
Defy both weather and the order to submit—
A stand of minutemen, bareheaded, stamping for dawn.

My father solemnly believed a God could live
Articulate in sumac and arbutus leaves;
That daily-witnessed death could be outrun
If once observed and written down. In sun, in rain,
I learned that duty and devotion are the same
When love and terror walk together. As the stream
Diverged, we stood on separate banks. He tried to show
Me where a red-eyed vireo might nest, the shy
Elusive whippoorwill might hide, but I could not
Distinguish anything except the wildest note
Of pity in their singing.

The shadblow's winter bark is grayish-green, and arcs
A double helix skyward like a double stair.
Its slender, ruddy, three-pronged twigs are mulberry
And beige, no bigger than my smallest fingernail.
The linden's lesions, caused by fungus and decay,
Have fissured vertically, the clawmarks parallel.
And rusty dogwood, tiled in ragged, reptilian plates,
Is sparring with its fuschia-colored, knuckled nodes.
The basket willow's tasseled catkins dangle in defeat,
Its twigs unraveling a yellow-greenish yarn.
The black trunk of a beech bristles its thousand wicks.
Today is a daguerreotype, tinted and brittle with loss.
Light dims the field. My fisted hands burn.
The crow shuffles its wings, arching over, is gone.

                    Palpably, the day
Was going. Twilight spilled the sky's embankment, dyed
On cloudy rungs cascading heaven's water wheel.
I saw the shadows joining hands, and all the while,
My father stood bewildered under Hesperus
And seemed to pray, I heard the birch's aspirates
Decline Monadnock's name; his, I think, and mine.
What called us? Was it something live or me that moaned?
He would not answer. Sickness burrowed every limb.
Our walks would fail. There was no resurrecting him.
But I have kept on walking, being tutored twice:
My father's daughter, trying to be spare, precise;
A child of earth, insistent on hell, on paradise.

v *Air*

Father, she's made the wolf a widower and orphaned us.
The world lies ruptured to the root, its harvest crushed
By her fallen heel, a maddened heaven thrashing white
Across her unforgiven dust, and shrouded elms weighted
In mourning. She who is dead teaches us grief, grieving
For us with a seraph's prayer and stylus, whose all-engraving
Trance transfixes us. Sleep has taken her up
Into its branches. She lets fall her shredded hope
Of treaties with the earth, regretting every flake's
Surrender. Dreamless in the shriven heart of oak,
Her thin, diminished breath collects until the day
When star-lichen studs the bark, a junco and chickadee
Will bear her back awake, willing herself young
Again, unpinning her hair, the river's rising song
Reviving us with mercy, in the water's tongue.

II

Last Year's Snow

for Susan Montbleau

I

Child's Play

His clothespin Grant had captured Lee
and where the Yankee Aubusson
was bloodiest, their armies lay
defeated in a clawfoot basin's
Boston fern, a cul-de-sac
of rebels in the jardiniere,
imaginary bivouacs,
so many wounds unburdened there.
He'd made the tender, fingered graves
of Appomatox, so his dead
could rest with simple childhood griefs,
where hope and all Virginia died.
A Lionel lay bushwhacked on
the desert near a milk-glass mesa,
and pygmy herds of chiseled bison,
unmolested, grazed a crayon map
where boredom stalled his planned assaults;
Comanche ponies drowsed with cavalry
and shared the prairie's peaceful grass.
The parlor light was charcoal gray.
Upholstered shadows were marooned
in static air. A thousand antimacassars
draped the lifeless furniture,
no other children playing there.

The piano's paisley shawl was fringed,
and made a dusky tent, a pirate's lair
where he could keep his hoarded
treasure trove: a hefty paperweight,
a globed duck's egg, which seemed to hold
the essence of winter; snow, a sleigh,

the steady changeless motion of its perfect sphere.
How could they make it storm inside the glass?
It swarmed like a quorum of white bees.
It quarreled in perfect silence,
baffling as those screen lovers
he saw with his aunt, Saturdays
in the balcony at the Rialto.
And when it slowed, it softened
to the dizzy descent of talc
in the ivory vapor of his bath.
It floated, as white paint flecked
his family's frescoed foyer,
the cherubs giving up their wings
one pinfeather at a time.
It was quieter than cedar or spruce
on the untobogganed face of Monadnock,
and seemed to shush itself for falling
as it fell, the way snow sank
on the pillowed Atlantic by the Cliff House
in winter and never made a sound.
It squalled over the sleigh, a crown of firs
and a fluted road which ran to the round horizon
and curved away, no matter how he chased it.
Daily, the blizzard turned from his hand.
The puzzle was magic. Snow dusted
the horse's muzzle with hoarfrost,
webbed her shaggy mane with ice.
It muffled the bridle and bright bit.
It undid straight lines scored by the runners' blade,
feathering the figures frozen to its lacquered floor.
The man in a fedora and weathered Chesterfield
was his father, whose mustache bristled
with impatience at his mother, in bisque,
who brushed her Lily Dache cloche
and cursed. He saw the white umbrellas

of their breath, their faces flash with argument
as snow salted their lashes. His throat was raw.
He saw his own whey face jawed
in a hound's-tooth collar, and became that child,
stuffed between his parents in a chilly January
where winter flaked its endless sorrow.
He stamped his boots to thaw his throbbing feet
and thought the pony, too, was shivering,
her glossy flanks imprisoned
in the stance of cantering.
Where would she take him on her marble hooves?
How far from the cold could they ride?
If he dropped her collar and breeching,
and slipped the traces from the whistle-tree,
they could shatter a thousand flying shards
above Broad Sound, startling the rigid
congregation of hymn-book brown boulders
over whose pages glazed with surf
winter's shaggy-bearded elders drowsed.
If he rubbed her nickering velvet lip,
if he leapt from the dash to her withers,
she would wake and race the shore
where the breakwater like a pastry shelf,
a tray of glass, upheld its frosted granite cakes.
Past Neptune, Mermaid, beyond Great Head,
Yirrell Beach and Deer Island, she would run
for the west where summer was
brushing her hair in a field of tansy and yarrow,
to browse in the humming yellow yawn
of sun, in timothy, in white clover.
Without halter or sleigh, she'd outrun the cold,
the ether'd trees, the brisk click
of lacquered nails on a powder box.
He'd strip off his stiff scarf,
wool hood, galoshes, leggings, stockings,

the fine gold *t* cradled on his collarbone.
Like a white swan, a gannet downed all in his flesh,
leaving them only a little volcano of clothes,
he would dive for her frothing mane
and ride the surf of her along the causeway,
his own hair like a flag. And his first night out
under the stars, though he'd know his way home
by those twinkling breadcrumbs, he'd build
a hero's fire, daring night to come for him.

But his mother would be crying in the lyre-back
chair beside the banjo clock, her bracelets
wrangling on the tambour sewing table,
his father roaring into his decanter.
Something flew in his eye, a grain, a seed.
He knew he could never ride ahead of the snow.
It would track him down.
A white hound would gnaw the leash
in his parents' yard, the rat-tat-tat
of its nails on the porch like hail.
He heard the hurricane of its coming,
the snarl of snow, he felt the growling
undergrowth stiffen and freeze.
Pebbles, pellets—he didn't know what they were,
or whether snow would suffocate or save him.
The owl of sorrow caught him like a mouse.
He was pressed in a linen apron, a muslin blouse,
smothered in an out'n flannel gown
and laid down. Snow fell like confetti—
someone had won something, someone
had been given away. Whiskey in a cup
was coddling him back, sunlight burned his lip
and choked him, but snow was soft,
patting his cheek like cat's paws.
He was safely tucked in his own bed.

The world's white hive released its whiter swarm.
What buzzed against the window's
queer cocoon? He pressed the glass.
He tasted braids of ice, as dwarfed
and dogged as a leafworm. It was cold.
He put his mittens on, and sighing,
drew a cotton sheet across his face.

II

The Bridegroom

His wedding morning woke him.
Fog hung over the shoulder of the coast,
a crony's sleeve, its headland nursing the tide
like a stevedore his stout. *Attar of roses.*
Lavendar. Lemon verbena. A guillotined mannequin
holding a cutaway coat. His beveled selves
were staggered in a pier glass triptych
above a pineapple maple bed and counterpane
where his aunts had slept out their great age,
and now lay across town in carved dressing gowns
where weather crossed out their names in needlepoint.
Organdy cringed at the window when he walked,
their mortified virgin ghosts appalled
at his body in their bed. He saw them young,
in their camisoles, waltzing
among chintzed armchairs,
watching for a sign of a man
or passion's whiskered cheek.
One wound the clock with a slender key,
the other turned down the gas.
Both crept graveward, paler every year.
The wounds that bleached them, unstanched,
stained pristine sheets, ripped from the bed
like calendar pages.
                    A faucet squawked.
The oval basin filled. Water ran over his hands
and woke him. She was an oread,
young June under a green awning,
daybreak, the thousand-voiced Squanicook
leaping a dam under willows,
September's roan-colored air,

each of her fingers lit by the quick flame
of her nails. She would never leave him.
Lather trembled on the shaving brush,
gathering in his beard like snow.
Gauzed, she would walk through a grillwork
of clear light, bearing a bouquet
of Eucharist lilies and stephanotis,
arriving in her storm of lace
to bend above the white lady's-cake
trimmed with silver drageés
and blade out their new portion.
Under its miniature canopy,
a waxen groom hands his organza'd bride
into a Christmas sleigh. She lifts her veil,
frost's delicate jacquard,
joining the reins in both her gloves:
they will go home under white candlewood,
white birch, white pine, white elm,
past laurel groves dusted with sugar
and white byrony's blood beading a satin bank.
A single snow bunting cajoles her invisible mate.
This time, they'll follow the fluted road,
and cross the chaste horizon,
a stream of wrought hexagons
under their bright-runnered sleigh.
Beyond the curve of seneschal firs,
a frosted cottage waits in winter air,
a granite step soon to be swept of powder
and the petals of his boutonniere.
Ice drops a lattice of morning glories
from the attic and the guttered eaves,
a glittering descant of welcome.
Her ivory bodice presses his waistcoat,
his wing-collar caught in the net of her hair.

Sweet Jesus, save me from her purifying nape
and the captive pearls parting the breasts
of an empress. One flake fell out of heaven
to melt on her moist lip, and shaken
from his revenant's gaze, he bent to bear
his love's white body over an oak threshold
where emptiness beat its hands and trembled
on the balustrade, tracing braille roses
the length of the papered hall,
the tissue of her gown shrouding his shoulder.
Organdy, crinoline, cambric, faille,
a Duchess satin chemise—layer by layer
she disrobed, as snow like swansdown
shivering from Leda's hand
covered the trees for shame.
A lighthouse, drawing up an apron
like a barkeep, winked a ribald eye
at all the passersby who hurled
fists of rice at the sills
until the very joists objected.
Sweet Jesus. Snow herded breakers shoreward,
the fleece of lambs hung on limbs to dry.
His skin surrendered where she kissed him,
his breath came out in plumes, frost etching
its intricate signature on his glass heart.

III

Armistice

Wind lay cradled in the dogwood's arms,
the sun stained its stroked bandages,
feverish above the treeline
as the body of the day was dying.
Stone by stone, Monadnock dimmed.
A regatta of clouds outsailed the dusk
across his room's great window.
A thousand brides who breached the dark
and bore their passions into sons
have mothered him, a thousand sons
have stood to plow their stony acre
for his sake. Polyneuritis, cirrhosis, pellagra—
timor mortis conturbat me.
What's left of his flesh is afloat on a white sheet,
water lapping the pilings at Litchfield's Wharf,
Cap'n Bergman piloting the *Brewster* by Graves' Light
and skirling smoke between snowbound harbor islands.
No. That can't be. The penny ferry no longer ran.
The WPA pulled down the piers before the War.
One of the wars. Some sea was rocking
his hospital bed, sailcloth weighted his limbs,
the rigging was running with blood.
A woman stood guard at his footrail,
one of the Pleiades in a white gown
who stepped down to earth
to bathe his face in snow.
Asperges me, my father.

So this is what the hurried river ran from,
why the phoebe grieved:
death with bourbon-colored hair

squeezing *aqua vitae* from a sponge.
He heard the bell tower toll in Metcalf Square,
a gargoyle grimacing as though a stroke
of ferrous light had wounded it.
And still she went on washing his hands,
a silent, snowblinding girl who stood by the hour,
too bright to be looked at long.
He wanted to sit up, to explain how the labors
of love had burdened him, and bad luck
dogged his every move, but light
was blizzarding about her face,
she was lifting away years of failure,
an adamant shroud. Once-healed scars
emblazoned on his skin awoke, and burned
to understand, and died again.
He felt the holy oils impoverish his eyes,
both hands and feet surrendering
to the snow's bright absolution
and the heartbeat of a linnet
persuading him to go. He heard the waters rising,
the Squanicook in her ragged aqueduct
on a furious run to the sea,
where the Tiber, Jordan, Lethe, Styx
converge. Past fields of rye, of barley,
his rafted spirit sailed, he drank,
as he had always done, to quench an earthly thirst
without an earthly remedy, and did forget,
and did lay down his animal bones,
all his incarnation self-consumed.

Fretting snow has gathered windrows
of Fessenden, Farrar, Dix, and moved aside
to put to rest, at a granite anagram,
the first of the season's casualties:
the child whose cradle rocked

when Argonne's candelabrum flared,
and Europe's hobnailed hurdy-gurdy
mortared up the organ pipes of princes,
a tide of excelsior flecking the hem
of a stone skirt in New York harbor,
and cases of treasure drifting home
with tattered glories hung from starboard and port—
here, all history shatters. I watch the Squanicook's
snared debris defeat the current,
as if the longer hand of time had beaten
the bruised hour in a duel, and victory
made tyrannical, made the minutes saunter.
Sabered cornrows freeze to honor him.
Requiescat, father. Day is done.
The Squanicook unlocks its jaws at last—
a peeling rowboat buoyed on the failing current
turns to commemorate the Armistice.
A sprinkling of bleached petals flakes
from the widow's hand at the oarlocks,
they ride the shallows under a stone bridge
where the shadows of seven soldiers site
November's opaque sky, and fire,
snow and shards of ice falling
for days across the shaken globe.

III

The Attic Bird

for Eleanor

I

New Year's Day 1986

Below a scalloped fanlight's leaded cames,
I pause and in the decades' doorway speak
the names of all my dead, who have become
alike as dust motes, drifting sunlit specks

illumined by the briefest hope of God,
despite the age's urge to die. As snow
ascends the printless steps with me, I'm glad
to have this landscape to myself on New

Year's Day. Resolved, my diction's fingertips
experiment along the windowledge,
and language fumbles with its latchkey, stopped
to hear the bolted couplings disengage.

How cavernous it seems, the empty hall
a century inhabited. The past
in shrouded furniture is glory's shell,
the chandelier and sconces wearing paste

about the throat and shoulders of the room
to prove that this occasion isn't grand,
their gems, in velvet, cached behind a brougham's
pair of Morgans and a picnic ground.

I haven't come to rob but reconcile
the way the dead were wounded with my blood.
What does a private history conceal?
And will it tell me why the decades bled?

With every step I climb, some kinship frets
its wings inside the cupola, a wren
or something in the house's heart, afraid
it can't get out. It beats so hard, I run

into the arid dormered eaves to free
whatever's captured there. But nothing live
is flailing, only a window shade that frayed
and fell. And through the broken valance, leaves

have blown and skitter on the floor like mice.
Or are they mice? Here are damaged stores
from sundered marriages, a wall-eyed moose
surveying the debris, his noble stare

not yet degraded by the moths that claim
his passive coat. A hundred frugal hands
have left their treasures here, and groaning, climbed
this steep, disordered passage toward their ends,

mortality breeding its own disease
in us, the wish to save, as if we had
a Pharaoh's endless afterlife to use
the objects where our terror learned to hide.

The dead survive without their furniture.
And I, who must inherit cherished rooms
of artifice, will be the family char
who cleans the house of everything but rhyme.

But something's caught my eye among the ruin—
an album, no, a velvet christening book,
half-mottled by a generation's rain.
The flyleaf is inscribed in faded black,

For my darling daughter, Eleanor;
the child who would become a matriarch,
formidable, tyrannical, inured
to any wishes but her own; and etched

beside her name, her birth commemorates
the birthdate of the century, *with love.*
And will I sanction what she writes?
And can her stories teach me how to live?

The page I puff on is a sheaf of ash,
where cinders start their candling of lines.
I shyly turn the pages of my flesh
and blood, writing for herself alone.

That child who cupped her chin and dreamt is dust.
Tongues and tribes have multiplied and died.
Ten thousand revolutions, unredressed,
have turned the sun's eye bloody, yet our dead
still write to us, and we are torn by what we read.

II

Easter 1900

Beyond the stiles, those rigid posts
where consonants and vowels roost
and serifs stir their wings, her past

has opened like a field, a maze
where complex briars decompose,
domesticated passions graze.

I read a delicate script describe
her growth: the hand-hewn hickory crib
was put away, her gums were rubbed

with clove. A mother's brief account
of joy reveals what facts cannot,
the moment's stereopticon:

"Oh, a glorious spring arrived
and brought your name, *Elnora Eve.*
Even the April sky approved.

The marble nave's forsythia
in Stoddard broke my heart, the air
so beautiful and golden there.

Your hand, a starfish, took my thumb.
The blessing stung. I heard the hum
of bees in lilies when your hem

was shivering against the font
like Queen Anne's lace above a pond.
We had a picnic on the lawn

beside the orchard. Father rocked
in a hammock hung between an oak
and Sheldon pear with you in the crook

of his arm, and all the fruit trees billowed
spring—the Northern Spy and Blue
Pearmain laid muslin out below

their limbs, the petals blew like snow,
and even our Seek-No-Further shows
a sign of bearing apples now."

III

Labor Day 1905

Edwardian simplicity,
that summer's wickerwork settee,
a gazebo under willow trees

where hours droned in leisurely flux,
the century's mill wheel winnowing flecks
of mica from gold—a time transfixed

by its reflection in a pool.
The pastoral's tempting idyll pulls
me back and makes the city pall

beside it. Honeyed light dissolves
the ghosts of poverty and saves
a garden with its virgin sylphs:

white lawn gowns and parasols,
a fragile paper boat that sails
the lesser Squanicook and stalls,

and where the shady ribbon runs,
two bridled horses doze, the roan
called Cherry Busco, rein-to-rein

and anchored to a white syringa
with her husband, Shadigay,
obedient to *haw* and *gee*

and *home.* In sweet blueberry grass,
on a blanket as they graze,
a child is softly singing, "Grace

abounding on the boundless sea"
knowing that the breezes sigh
because the summer cannot stay.

It is a temporary peace,
this picnic gotten for a price
by Knights of Labor and police,

from fireworks and men that boast
their stones' and nightsticks' volley burst
above the scabs' and strikers' breasts.

IV

Thanksgiving 1908

A child, abruptly, years ago,
awoke and heard her name, its echo
inaugurating sense. Her ego

shook itself from innocent sleep
to comprehend the palpable shape
of a woodshed and cooper shop

where farm machinery chained to the wall
was alive and had a steely will
of its own. A kitten's caterwaul

astonished her under the nail kegs. Each
implement in its gloomy niche
was forged for use—a goose-wing broadax

and lathing hatchet, barrel staves
hooped on a peg, an Ashley stove's
six-lidded top and damper starved

for polish near a pomace rake,
upended in a broken hayrack.
A mud wasp's nest in firebrick

festooned with harnesses that coiled
like snakes. Old snaths and sickles, scaled
by spiders, crowned a toothless scroll

saw, and where a fallen cleaving froe
had ploughed a mound of grain, a farrow
of spotted piglets scratched the furrow.

54

A chestnut cider cask, a still,
sticky with mother of vinegar, swelled
the dooryard's step where biddies strolled

to coax a strutting bantam cock.
She heard the pond's encomium, the croak
of grandfather bulls, the winching creak

of sugar maple boughs, but all
that passed for industry—unoiled—
collapsed, corroded, bled. The well

and well sweep drowned in sycamore.
The shed, a shingled sway-back mare,
was put to pasture. Mice admired

shadow-mice in troughs where rain
ignored a gutter of fledgling wrens
and ivy's impenetrable runes.

The only men were made of straw
and tethered to that place, destroyed
by work and luck—the scarecrow's true

inheritors who left their doors
ajar, where hooves of browsing deer
had hammered milkpails in the dew.

As stickmen watched a phantom road
go by, their flesh in rags, they prayed
they owned the land, or stood with pride,

thanksgiving for a scrawny fowl,
squawking headless through the field,
for all the famine they had fled.

V

Columbus Day 1910

Papa took us to New York.
We climbed inside the Lady. We walked
a million stars. Not *stairs,* the dizzy
stresswork helix riveting blowsy
matrons, brats agog in shirtwaists
and sailor suits whose white wrists
ran with chocolate from forgotten
cones, all quibbles dwarfed by her titan
struts. One hundred fifty-four
bewildering steps, a flight of fired
rungs a Jacob might have groped
where pilgrims swarmed like wood lice, gaped
downward at the star-shaped deck,
marveling at the little ferry docked
so far below them. The city slipped
under clouds as furious wind slapped
the copper skin and howled its other-
worldly grief around them, and either
fear or perfect happiness pumped
her ten-year-old heart. What prompted
panic wasn't clear. She'd arched
and was dreaming, afloat, her body perched
like Jingo, her father's ancient parrot.
She leaned like a figurehead on a pirated
schooner, imagining Bermuda's open
azure and sailing away from the pine
island, home; where instead of snow
hibiscus blew, and only new
turtles disturbed the sand, and no one
bickered in the languid lap of noon.
A sudden gull squawked close

to the casement. Its black eye pierced
her with vertigo. It hated her, that eye,
it hated fiercely, black as the boy
who'd crouched to shine their shoes and hawked
tobacco at her skirt as they hiked
Times Square. Something wicked laughed
in its breast, malevolence lifted
its wing and flew away.
                              At ten,
steaming toward Manhattan, a tin
figure stiff on the blurred horizon,
stony and grave, she'd kept her eyes on
the iron sunburst, the torch's receding
flame, all the while reciting
a rosary of nonsense rhymes that wind
and the layering swells swallowed, word
after word, the feeble flotsam and jetsam
she'd spat on the cheek of a wave. Those same
stone lids would seek her out
one day, the vast protruding foot
would crush a doorsill. Death had a giant's
hand and would carve *Eleanor* in granite
too, her jaw a glacier, her mouth
a precipice.
                    Months later, a moth's
blundering track feelered the face
of her grief on the clammy page, her fist
gripping the Biltmore's pen, forced
to write *Mama's dead* first
followed by *I'm having a new dress
made*. I see her in the cheval glass,
trembling on the seamstress's stool
in eyelet bloomers, hearing steel
blades scissor a pinafore;
raspy Caruso's mechanical furor

matched by that Canuck soprano, sops
of *ma pauvre p'tite* and marzipan shaped
into hearts. Surprising sunlight spilled
through mullioned windows. Neon spelled
confusing prisms on brick. She reeled
from breathing pomade in parted rolls
of hair, skewered in rats on the scalp
of the clucking seamstress, bent to sculpt
the pleated collar into place. A circlet
of rodents' teeth, those pins, an amulet
of flame. White-faced, the child cringed,
a live thread in the shears' hinge
ending it. A mannequin dressed, dowered.
Under the comet, as good as dead.
The crowded harbor's daylight fails,
the little ferry *Astrophel*
where the Europes disembark
sinks, exhausted, at the dock.

VI

Christmas 1912

I grow conscious of her script
as she had done. It struggled for poise.
And something had bled the ink—it crept
away from her tentative strokes, the O's

covering their mouths. Whatever mist
first blurred the lines returns to be read,
the letters failing faint ghosts
of hollyhocks that nudge a grid

of pasture fence, witnessing the wild
lilies' long migration, the deep
declivities of love. A startling world
reveals itself, the way a drop

of ordinary water leaps
to life under its proper lens.
I fix my eye, a jeweler's loupe,
on a half-familiar girl, my glance

exhuming every stripe her blind
emotion made, each sharp stroke
of teal-blue ink a needling blond
engraver's fierce tatoo that streaks

my paper skin. I read the handprints
of my dead on rain-soaked walls,
a rooftree forging their old complaints—
pebbles, sounding a stygian well.

VII

St. Patrick's Day 1914

Her voice is clear though she disguised
her paddocked heart with lilac sprays,
entangling her deep disgust.
Electric as a fence, her prose

is wired lightning cinched by rage.
It stings my hand, as hers was stung.
I part her clotted foliage
and follow my surveyor's string,

an archaeologist who sorts
through layered, fragmented debris.
From what she wrote in fits and starts,
I draw imagined gold from brass.

I think I see the peeling newel
of her father's house, the porch
aligned against a tipsy knoll
and scabrous roof where starlings perched.

Behind her prickly gate of words,
I sketch her boundaries and roads,
a hundred acres stretching toward
Bellwether Hill where stoneboats rid

the field of stumps; a stubborn oak
and sumac's semaphore; the bay-
berried backhouse where an uncle, drunk,
had nailed a sign, "Ah! Here It Be!"

But snow was endless in Vermont,
the snow of legend. April's war
with March, a raid of tulips, meant
a truce at best, in places where

stalactites blade the eaves' knife-
rack or trumpet vine taps a downspout,
impatient, ancestral, waiting to know if
the guilty would hang or time deport

survivors. All through Lent she camped
in a tiny borning room beside
the winter kitchen, quarters scrimped
and patched by what the old man said

was thrift: an object that had arms
and legs still had its use. She wrote
by lamplight, cursed the senseless form
his hoarding took—wrought-iron rat-

tail hinges piled in a nest; a piggin
of nails; a caudle cup crammed with brads;
her petticoat's gnawed hem plugging
the wainscot. Clutter was his bread

and meat, he feasted on the spoils
of some imagined feud the world
began, whose broken treasure spilled
in coffers flung from Fortune's wheel.

Some sadistic seamstress stitched
her winding cloths across the ell
and lintel, draping selvedge etched
in coquillage of ice, till all

the windows filled with flannel light.
A single fire blushed, and stoked
to ash, the supple limbs had lit
chaotic triumph's random stacks.

Her sleep was full of murder where
a shack was blazing on a cliff,
the door would jam. Once, she swore
she'd turned into the weaning calf,

an animal bewildered in its hood
of iron spikes, thrashing down
the sugar orchard's gate, who hurled
itself against the bars till dawn.

VIII

Valentine's Day 1916

For years a pair of cherubs dallied
there, the ink turned aubergine
above their curls, the faithful office
of their wings. A link of lace
was powder where their hands had joined,
the heart's original magenta dulled

to bloodless rose. The mystery,
desire, tucked away, redeemed
her notion of another time,
abandoned artifacts entombed
before her parents' love was damned
in rose-leaves' fragile potpourri.

From attic raids, her cedar bridebox
slowly filled with relics, eased
in secret from a musty clothespress,
not the kind of theft a priest
could censure—they were hers because
they'd been her mother's first: an onyx

brooch, the bolts of Devonia lace,
the wheat-colored cuffs in *broderie
anglaise;* and nearly lost behind
a chimney in a trunk, the hand-
done water color of a dairy
maid, dressed in a brown pelisse.

Some amateur who'd never trudged
manured cow paths painted it.
Imagination made her face
unearthly. Laden pails, her fists,
deceptive moonlight hinted at
a wending toward some tragedy.

The girl was bound to think sometimes
it was her mother on the road
by Colby Hill, hearing the wheels
of his democrat scrape the gravel, swirls
of love-in-the-mist at her hem. But would
he come this time with his strapping team

to take her home? Could she, the last
firelight flushing her cheek, not say
husband, come to bed; in the hurricane
lamp's obscuring glass become
the dairy maid, seeing the child who sees
herself there, and their palimpsest?

IX

The Fourth of July 1918

The governor's son commanded pages
as war stormed the ruled horizon,
unplaiting Sunapee and pledges
made in summer's first frisson.

Forbidden love, she'd written twice,
at first for joy, and then for grief.
Did she find her supple waist
disturbing, or her breasts, the grave

and perfect sweetness of her lips
bewildering because he'd found
them beautiful? In her slip,
she saw what prohibition fanned.

As Warren with a single laugh
collapsed her like a house of cards,
the farm and all its dust sheets luffed
and sank below the peak of Kearsage—

desire and his finger touched
the chokecherry curve of her mouth—a thousand
tethers loosed, her heart detached
a delicate kite on the wind's ascent,

she was caught in a lark's-head hitch,
a tender half-blood-knot, his hands.
July's Mare Meadow was their church,
and she, a languid, daisy-chained

new bride, nibbled on sassafras,
whistling through the fisted blade
that split their fathers' angry frieze,
a root much older, more wayward than blood.

And what they stole from summer held
when August stalked the goldenrod
and autumn in his arms, enthralled,
shook down her hair upon the road.

His dogtags gently brushed her face,
her heart seceded from the farm
for his otherearthly flesh,
a brown-eyed boy in uniform

who, suddenly, was riding off.
The letters. Then the Telegram
she burned, his passionate words a puff
of smoke, her paper heart a simulacrum.

X

Decoration Day 1920

Old mother May has put her burden down.
Her heavy-headed poppies drowse where flags
and epaulettes of crepe across the stones
still will us to our bandaged dead, those flocks
of innocents eternally ordained
to die. *And all of them were captains, stained
by circumstance.* In veils, the widow stands
to hear a downy bugler grieve, adorned
by glory's ribbon which his spittle flecks.

She married fear and bore a son, with drums
repeating indistinctly in her blood
some requiem, the wounds of winter closed
by tearful June; a willow in her braids,
she sits astride a pasture fence and dreams
the gateway opens, ankles tightly laced,
still kicking, inconsolable; at last
engendering a grandchild who could rhyme
and fist her fury's fiercely hoarded blade.

How terrible that *savor* lost a limb,
becoming *save;* that with it, *safety* went.
She spied behind each specter-bolted door
her ancient, fearsome adversary *want,*
his thousand henchmen threatening to climb
some unprotected window chink. What dire
calamities she made her heart endure
ahead of time, a tethered matted lamb
before the slaughter, terrified of wind.

Her house is sagging now, the rafters propped
with lolly columns. Here, her doubt once piled
these rotted boxes, curtains, buttons, rags.
This attic lurching from the past has pulled
its peddler's wagon, years severely roped
together, tented by its threadbare rug.
She only kept alive her miser's rage.
The seeds she saved could not be sown and reaped.
Is it death or me that stands here more appalled?

It's me, my wings which beat against the glass,
a songbird in a magpie's nest that calls
uncertainly. All nature says *lift up,*
rejoice. The dead are brooding in their cowls
for blood, their eloquence is pitiless.
Between the sunshook foliage, my hope,
and shadows of the dead I cannot help,
I thrash exhausted at the bars and lose
my voice, the world dissolving in this cell.

I've done with legacies, all striped by welts
of war, and dare myself to die, infirm
and greedy as my kin, when in my eyes
there rises up a slender, laughing form,
and suddenly my resolution wilts—
my lover, Wilfred Owen, threads the maze,
death's honor guard, lieutenant to the Muse,
who'll bend me in our consonantal waltz,
and take me down to dinner on his arm.

IV

The Housewright's Mercy

for Rick and Joyce

i

I heard the apples softly letting go
at summer's end, and knew abundance drowsed
beside me in the field, her freckled arm
flung wide above her headscarf, while a dream
of cider filled the Nonesuch cheeks with rust.
They tumbled from her apron, fully grown.
A sparrow, mating with its echo, bred
a fledgling music. I was no one's bride.

Who knows why summer broke my heart that year?
September always said *too ripe, too ripe.*
In Hubbardston, the world was threshing gold,
my brother's acres far too light-beguiled
for herds or harvesters. And who could reap
the hillsides, flecked with such excelsior?
Oh Lord, I couldn't pray, as language asks.
I was too small, and autumn's only husk.

And when some worm deranged itself in me,
I thought I couldn't live to watch the light
inevitably yield. A thread, a hair
was all that held me to the earth that hour—
invisibly plucked from her golden head, she laid
redemption in my hands. A scythe might mow
the meadow now. I saw that both my life
and death would matter less than any leaf.

I sat alone, an anvil's shadow, as
five workmen pounded on my brother's house.
Their awkward, fitful battering on brick,
on granite, pinned me to the apple bark,
their hammers thundered wood the way a horse's
fired hooves bombard its stable doors.
I heard in their harangue of wrists a flash
of judgment, and their gavels nailed my flesh.

A pause. Then on the scaffolding I felt,
like rowers straining toward some far-off shore,
their purpose forge a single instrument,
I heard one hammer's rhythm, adamant
with joy—it found the root of work in sheer
exertion, making, as the rafters filled
with iron on the clapboards' stave, both song
and signature where men have moved as one.

And as they beat in harmony, I thought
a cloud of sawdust half-eclipsed the sun.
The hammers slowed to match my heartbeat while
their shapes upon the ridgepole dimmed. And veiled
by cooler, unfamiliar light, with sand
the mind can worry pearlward in my throat,
their restoration stood for all we make
in life, and all that perishes like smoke.

The New House, 1802

I saw how Joseph Wright would heft his ax,
Wachusett, Asnacomet, Burnshirt Hill
still wilderness, his Great Farm Thirty-Two
a parchment blot, a Monarch's dribbled tea.
He'd trace two Georgian parlors, limn a hall,
an ell, his carriage shed and barn. With sticks
to mark the cornerposts and piers, he'd pace
an arch where wagonloads of hay would pass.

He'd hear the oxen snake a sawyer's sledge
through clotted undergrowth, his timber roar
a snowy skidway to the stack, where sills
were hewn and sawn a season later. Soil,
uncovered by the carted oak and briar,
in bloom with every limb the team dislodged,
would flake with cedar woodchips to his shins.
He'd watch the drawshave's resin gild his hands.

The master mason's shyest son would stoke
a beehive oven, full of firebrick,
until he dropped. But stung because the Dutch
were libeled there, he'd dig a man-sized ditch,
then supervise the cradling of rock,
each hoisted hearthstone guided by his stick.
He'd blush and bend to lift his palanquin
of clay. They'd use his tempered bricks, in quoins.

The mason, topping out the chimney course
and waving like a weathercock, would toss
his trowel down and drop his scutch and hod.
His chimneys pointed heavenward. They had
proportion. They would conquer even trees.
Extinguished at the firedogs with cares
of men, the wood and not his flues would fail
when sparrows, nestling in the thimble, fell.

And though they knew their carpentry was good,
the men would flinch to think he'd find a flaw,
and wipe their boots, afraid to enter rooms
that they themselves had built. He'd diagrammed
this balustrade and stairs. The wainscot. Floors
of twenty-two inch pine, like planks of gold.
He'd thumb the latch, a man afraid to wake,
and touch his tricorn, grateful for their work.

She'd stand, like Ruth among the gleaners, broom
in hand, to clear the shavings' chaff from wheat.
Their house was built. A landlocked brigantine.
The hipped roof. Elegant. The downspout, turned
where fascia boards and soffits met. The weight
of stories borne by joists and summer beams.
He'd proudly stroke a pilaster. Then carve
his *Boaz,* just above the fanlight's curve.

iii

The Widow, 1819

But building such a house would kill him. Now
I see their marriage candle—Martha Wright
would rock in her bedroom window, facing west,
for twenty years without him and would twist
her hair, a braided flame, in figure eights,
entwining all the sorrows women know.
The moon in popular trees, her ivory comb,
a world away, she'd weep as evening came.

When Joseph Wright wed Martha Eveleth,
briefly, briefly, as the fiddler sang,
the apple trees themselves wore periwigs,
and crows in frock coats settled battles waged
by cedar fencepost statesmen, witnessing
their declaration of intent. A myth:
it was not fruit that tempted Adam but
the deeply moonlit orchard's featherbed.

Thus passion's mill wheel ladled out their Sabbaths.
On fevered linen, spent by love and quarrels,
as quickly as she healed, her body writhed:
their blue-eyed Joab, Aaron, earnest Ruth;
Chloe, Sally, Nathan, Bildad, Charles;
the babies, quiet Catherine, Dorcas, Beth.
What piercing joy to have it all again:
his whisper *moppet,* then her lying-in.

They grew like summer saplings while their hair,
those fields of wheat the wind might gently part,
would darken at the milkroom door. She'd chalk
their crowns, her fingers tethering their cheeks,
and measure what another season spared.
How good God was. And then she wasn't sure:
her fallen willow, Sally, flailed a week;
her first-born Joab struck down like an oak.

Mortise-and-tenon. Post-and-beam. She'd trace
her husband's drawings in her sleep—a home,
a virgin house, a ghostless place where plagues
of earth would never come, a farm, built leagues
from grief. In Hubbardston, the saw pit hummed
where mists at evening service through the trees,
her fevered logic like an invalid's,
were children, by the elders, being led.

Crocus. Cowbells. Leaf-fall. She'd mistake
each season's alchemy for happiness.
Their first December froze so deeply, graves
could not be dug. The cistern of her grief
encased in stone her daughter Chloe, next
to Joseph, dead within a week of stroke.
I see a tundra through their window cracks,
and northern lights, still burning as she rocks.

iv

Her widowhood was one long labor, piled
like cordwood in the shed. Her patience streamed
through fallow fields, on sun-struck corn, a scythe,
in geese disconsolately going south.
A miller, plowman, smith and cooper stormed
the farm, her full-grown sons; her daughters pulled
down linen, fresh from apple boughs, to press
the housewright's relict back to earth, in peace.

I thought I saw the clapboards pale, as though
the house itself could mourn for Martha Wright,
but it was snow, a thousand nor'east gales
that blew above a shipwreck—furied gulls
new generations of neglect had brought.
The timbers groaned. The shingles warped with thaw.
Defeated by its never-ending chores,
no legal owner was his rightful heir.

His hayfields stand like beggars at the gate
and startle reptiles in the ferns. The roots
of one remaining wine-glass elm succumb
as ivy splits the shattered fanlight's cames.
A shutter bangs. Powder-post beetle routs
the summer beams where Queen Anne's lace forgets
itself and leans like Puritan children toward
a gibbet or a pulpit or their God.

I knew what Joseph Wright had known, what drove
each hand-made nail: *no marketplace could price
such beauty. Sons must fence themselves apart.*
But through the dusk, his vision half-impaired,
empowered by the things of earth to praise
the earth, the housewright saw our love, derived
from his; who chose this lifetime's enterprise,
as artists' work—by work—is best appraised.

My brother wants a visionary's house,
and reads and signs the housewright's master plan:
in what we leave behind, a chiseled script,
we ask for mercy's constant care, to keep
our names alive. This verse I've tried to plane
for strangers, hewn as faithfully as his,
this home I build, the labor of my life,
must be a place in which the world can live.

Who knows what heaven is? Or if we're left
with Joseph shouldering his ax, the girth
of ringed infinity's elm—to try and glimpse
through darkness Martha's incandescent lamps.
Does broken Carthage most resemble death,
or do those workmen on the roof who lift
a horizontal beam, stripped to the waist,
still forge the final crosspiece of the West?

WRIGHT LIBRARY
1776 FAR HILLS AVE.
DAYTON, OHIO 45419

02948